FOR MARILYN MUELLER

In March 2021, my mom, Marilyn Mueller, passed away unexpectedly. She loved art in all its forms, and was always creating and teaching. She was a voracious reader, and was often reading at least three books at one time. She was a brilliant and generous storyteller who wrote two children's books. While her children's book, "Giant Sunflowers," was not published during her lifetime, it is featured in the pages of "Giant Sunflowers Journal I" and "Giant Sunflowers Journal II." In addition to honoring her memory, my hope is that it will inspire you to read, write and tell the stories that are in your heart.

Happy creating,

Heidi

Heidi Mueller
Founder of Excelsior Candle Co.
Co-Founder of Founders Co.

GIANT SUNFLOWERS JOURNAL I & II

© Copyright 2023 Heidi Mueller and Chris Olsen

ISBN: 979-8-9883444-0-7 (I)
ISBN: 979-8-9883444-1-4 (II)
Printed in the United States of America
First Printing: 2023

Published by Publish Her, LLC
2909 South Wayzata Boulevard
Minneapolis, MN 55405
www.publishherpress.com

Cover art by Kayla Franz

PUBLISH **HER**™

GIANT SUNFLOWERS
By Marilyn Mueller

The shimmer of the summer morning sun on the lawn made the dewdrops twinkle as if tiny diamonds were attached to each blade. Meadowlarks in the tall spruce trees lining Heidi's yard welcomed the day with their happy song.

The animals in the nearby woods were also waking to the new day. Deer cautiously stepped out of the piney forest, sniffing the air to search for any danger and then lowering their tan heads to nibble at the thick green vegetation in the meadow.

A red fox loped out of the thistly juniper trees and stopped to scratch his rust-colored ear before heading to a raspberry patch for his breakfast. It was this fox's favorite early morning hangout, and he was there every day.

June had arrived at last, and this was the first day of summer vacation. Heidi lay in her bed watching the golden rays of sun peek around her window shade and melt across the pink walls of her bedroom.

Every summer, Heidi had her own spot in the garden to plant whatever she wanted to grow. During past summers, she had grown sweet potatoes, popcorn, green beans, peanuts and sunflowers. This summer, she was going to plant sunflowers again. But not just ordinary sunflowers, GIANT sunflowers. Ten-foot-tall sunflowers, to be exact. That was what was printed on the seed package. Heidi thought about the sunflowers she had planted before. They were tall, but not that tall!

Heidi had loved visiting the garden in the morning to see their large brown faces and yellow petals pointing toward the morning sun in the east. As the sun made its way across the sky, the sunflower heads would follow its path west, facing the setting sun at night. Heidi would visit the opposite side of the garden every evening. It was fun to see the flower heads changing direction with the sun. It was why they were called sunflowers.

Heidi and her mom planted the giant sunflowers after reading the directions on the seed package. First, they took a trowel and made a long furrow in the rich, dark garden soil. They got down on their hands and knees and placed the seeds in each row. Heidi crawled along the rows and carefully covered them with dirt.

Next, they put marker sticks at the end of each row, so they knew exactly where the seeds were planted. Heidi took the seed package and attached it to one of the marker sticks, so she knew those markers were for her sunflowers.

Heidi put the sprinkler in the garden to water her seeds. Then she waited and watched for the warm earth and water to bring the sleeping seeds to life. After about 10 days, she noticed tiny green stalks with two leaves each that had pushed their way out of the ground. Some of them had sprouted so quickly that the black-and-white striped shell of the sunflower seed hung from the new leaves like tiny ornaments.

The sunflowers needed water, sunshine, fertilizer and careful weeding to help them grow, and grow they did. The summer passed quickly, and the warm summer days and rainfall at night helped them flourish. The seed package had been right. The giant sunflowers were 10 feet tall. Their huge golden-brown heads were so heavy with seeds that they bent over slightly. With their thick green stems and elephant-ear-sized leaves, they looked as if they belonged in the jungle instead of Heidi's garden.

When people drove past the garden, they would slow down and stare at the giant sunflowers. Heidi was very proud of her sunflowers. She planned to leave them to dry in the fall so that when winter came and blanketed the ground in white, her giant sunflowers would feed the birds and wild animals that came into the yard. Then she would have plenty of time to dream of what she would plant next year.

Tell the stories
that are in
your heart.